DATING CHRONICLES OF A TRAVELING

NOMAD: RECOLLECTIONS OF THE

FUNNIEST, CRAZIEST, AND MOST

MEMORABLE DATING EXPERIENCES

Leila McSalle

ISBN: 0998376604
ISBN-13: 978-0998376608

CONTENTS

INTRODUCTION

Once upon a time, there lived a sassy girl, full of passion and exuberance with a zeal for exploration and trying new things. This sometimes led her to the unlikeliest of places with the most unusual people. It wasn't until sharing some of the craziest and wildest stories of dating excursions with her best friend and others, that it dawned on her that other people might actually be amused by her experiences.

In this book, I give an account for some of the most interesting men I've dated. Some of the situations are funny; others could have been downright dangerous, but what's life without taking chances? Every single detail, as unbelievable as some might seem, has happened over a 10-year span. I do not attempt to teach profound philosophical lessons or preach like many online dating books. Rather, I'm just sharing a few of my lighthearted dating experiences that make a good coffee table read.

1 THE YOUNG & THE TOOTHLESS: DENNIS

I've always been curious, delving into things that seemed novel and mysterious. This transcended well into adulthood, and the then new phenomenon of online dating happened to pique my interest. It's a bit hard to fathom now considering how commonplace it is for everyday couples to have met online, but way back when chat rooms just began to gain popularity, people for the most part were embarrassed to say they met someone online. This did not deter me, but rather made the concept even more enticing.

I was about 16 years old when a particular young man and I met in a chat room and started corresponding. He seemed interesting and funny, so we exchanged numbers and spoke for hours on end everyday. A few months later, I decided that I would do something exciting and meet him in real life. All kinds of emotions ran through my head. I was highly skeptical of meeting anyone from the Internet, so I asked a few of my girlfriends to join me. I had no car at the time, so our close proximity made our meet-up very convenient.

We exchanged pictures (this was before Skype or "web camming" reached its peak) and all had seemed well.

I only received two pictures from him—one of him smiling with his mouth closed and the other with a hat on. Nothing in particular struck me as odd or suspicious so to speak. I remember being super nervous, but I didn't necessarily have high hopes. I had never had a boyfriend before, so I wasn't exactly sure what to expect.

I gleefully walked to the agreed-upon location with a group of my friends. They stood far enough away for him not to know they were with me, but close enough to keep an eye on me, just in case.

I saw him before he saw me. I had to rub my eyes a few times to ensure I was seeing correctly, but he had described what he would be wearing in detail so I knew it was him. Much to my chagrin, he only had about six teeth! Then it became abundantly clear why he didn't smile in any of his pictures. He also had a weird haircut, high-water pants, beat-up sneakers, and a faded Hawaiian shirt. My jaw hit the floor! I thought I'd be able to escape before he saw me, but no such luck. He said "hello" to which I promptly said "good-bye!" With my eyes wide open in shock, I swiftly ran for it. To make matters worse, my girlfriends saw him too. They laughed uncontrollably as they watched me bolt. I never felt bad about leaving the scene, because certain information should not be withheld (e.g., being damn near toothless). This was the moment I decided I was not going to meet another person online without seeing them on their webcam first.

2 CASE OF THE EX: LIAM

When I was about 18, I found myself at one of the most vulnerable points in my life. My first love and I had broken up several months before, and I was seeking something reminiscent of the connection and good times of my prior relationship. I often would use the Internet as the quickest means to meet people. As a senior in high school, I never liked the idea of dating someone in my own school where there'd be a lack of privacy. Besides, I had a penchant for older men. In many cultures, it's acceptable for men to be way older than the women, and I always felt I had an old soul that related better with people older than me. That's when I met Liam. Liam and I would talk until the wee hours of the morning about anything and everything. I don't exactly recall how it came up, but he told me he was separated. I had no idea what that meant at the time. I believed him when he said he wasn't with his wife anymore, given how much we would speak every day.

When volunteering information about his wife (I never really asked), he described what she looked like and how she was verbally and emotionally abusive toward him when he was overweight. He also gave me a sob story of how she had cleaned out their bank account and he somehow found out she was on some dating website and cheated with over 30 men (or so he claimed). It took a while for us to meet in real life (I didn't have a car at the time). When we finally had our first date, I was less than impressed. I don't know if it was nervousness or what, but he was too weird—the way he ate his food and his odd mannerisms. He took the smallest nibbles out of his food that I'd ever seen, and he ever so delicately held his knife and fork to cut up the contents on his plate, as if he felt the vegetables had feelings and he was softening the blow. And then he lovingly gazed at his drink, as he took miniature sips, as if never wanting it to finish (the funny thing is refills were free). By the end of the night, it was obvious no sparks had flown.

He did the infamous "fade out" after our date for a few weeks (complete radio silence), but then suddenly, he reappeared again. When he finally called me back, I could hear a lot of commotion in the background as he had company over, and then he uttered some disrespectful things to show off in front of his friends. I dare not repeat what he said, but let's just say it caused me to promptly tell him off and hang up the phone. That was that—or so I thought.

I never have and still don't completely trust the Internet or social media. Eventually, I created a MySpace account with tight security settings; only people who knew my email address (which I didn't give out all willy nilly) could find me. One day, out of the blue, I received a random message from a woman I didn't know. Intuitively though, I knew exactly who she was as soon as I read the first line:

Hi, I'm a friend of Liam. He told me the two of you dated and I was wondering what was he like? I've been hurt several times before and I am just curious to know about his character.

Mentally, the whole situation triggered a recollection of Liam's loose description of his wife (ethnicity wise), and she fit the bill. It became very obvious why their marriage was so dysfunctional—no one knew how to tell the truth. It was peppered with lies and deception.

It made me very mad to see she would lie to me and then insult my intelligence on top of it. Had she come to me woman to woman, I would have had no qualms telling her we mainly spoke on the phone and had only one pathetic date. She chose to be dishonest, so I chose not to comply. Considering the only way I could be found on MySpace was through my email, I gathered she probably badgered him into giving her my email or she snooped and found it. He wasn't on my MySpace friends list, nor did we have mutual friends, so her lies were pretty blatant. I figured she most likely asked him what happened between us while they were separated, he told her, she didn't believe him, so she had an asinine plan to get "the truth" herself by telling lies. I decided to reply:

I know exactly who you are. Anything and everything you need to know, you need to ask your husband, Liam. I am not telling you anything.

She was pretty irate at this point.

How does it feel to have been a concubine? You messed with a married man, which is the lowest of lows! He told me you were ugly and looking at your picture, I would definitely agree. He also told me you tried to make moves on him but he didn't oblige. We are happy now and he has now become an honest man.

I found her self-righteous, inane drivel hilarious to the utmost degree. Here was someone who allegedly cheated on her husband with over 30 men and depleted their joint bank account thinking she was "holier than thou;" comedy at its best. It was also laughable that I was so ugly and horrible that (a) He felt the need to even mention me considering we only went on one insignificant date two years prior (b) I was so ugly that he went out with me in the first place and she felt threatened enough to contact me. I couldn't deal with her immaturity any longer so my final rebuttal was:

How does it feel to be 10 years my senior and harassing me?

Does that make you feel like a woman? He told me many things about you as well that I am not going to repeat. If your relationship is perfect and he is the exemplary husband, then bask in that bliss and leave me alone. I am blocking you so this is the end of this conversation. Good luck and God bless!

Thankfully, I never heard from either party ever again. I learned very quickly what "separated" really meant and from that point onward, I never voluntarily ventured into those murky waters.

3 THE CHEAPSKATE: NELSON

Nelson was a man I had met on the dating website hotornot.com. He was a handsome Italian man and an established commercial jingle-writer in the Big Apple. He was about 24 and wanted to meet up in person. At that time, I generally liked to speak to someone regularly for at least two weeks before meeting. I never have, and still don't like feeling rushed when meeting a person from online.

I suppose the first red flag should have been the fact that Nelson told me his longest relationship only lasted four months. I don't remember the reason he gave for that particular break-up, but I do remember thinking it seemed trivial.

Nelson was a braggart, and it annoyed the hell out of me. I thought that would be the least likable aspect of his personality, but by the end of our first date, I was proven wrong. There was a worse character trait to be unveiled, especially considering all the information (I didn't ask about) that he elected to reveal.

Apparently being a hot shot in his field afforded him luxuries such as an upscale, $5,000 a month apartment next to the Empire State building. He told me all the details of the superb amenities and how exclusive and expensive the complex was. During our first meet-up, he nagged me into visiting his apartment. I had never gone to anyone's place on a first date, so I was very reluctant. After emailing his photo and information (including his address) to my best friend, I agreed. I didn't even step two feet into the door before the boasting began.

"Nice to finally meet you, Leila!"

"Likewise. You know, I've never gone to the apartment of a guy I barely knew on the first date. I'm a little nervous and hope I'll be ok."

"Don't be silly, Leila; you're in safe hands. Check out my sweet pad."

"How beautiful is the view, the skyline and patio? This apartment is awesome. And right next to the Empire State building too. My brother and I pay about $5,000 a month to live here! Pretty expensive but why not? You see that rug over there? $2,000. This place has a bellman and all these wonderful amenities," said Nelson, as he gleefully gave me a tour of his not-so-humble abode.

He then continued, "I love what I do, writing jingles! I must say, I'm pretty good at it! I've written them for Sony, Toyota, Apple, and a bunch of other big name brands. I even have a YouTube channel with over 200,000 views." He then proceeded to whip out his phone, to "prove" he did in fact have 200,000 views on his YouTube page.

"I make a lot of money writing jingles. I have about two jobs lined up this week."

Bear in mind, I never asked him any questions about his finances or anything financially related; he volunteered all of this information. He also didn't ask me much about my job, or even *just about me in general*, and I couldn't get a word in edgewise.

The night before our date, he had made some food that he was very proud of. I didn't feel comfortable accepting food or drinks that could have been spiked or

God knows what else beforehand, so I politely declined. It's almost insane I know, how I take greater chances yet become guarded when it comes to smaller ones.

We ended up leaving the apartment and going to my favorite pizza place. We went in line, and I started to order some pizza. The cashier looked at my date and asked if our order would be separate or together. He shook his head, saying he wouldn't be ordering anything. However, as soon as I paid for my food, he pulled a douchebag move and ordered food for himself less than a minute later (I kid you not). Apparently he found greater pleasure in bragging about his $5,000 a month apartment than being a gentleman and paying for his date's food on the first date.

If he hadn't ordered any food or even waited until we sat down and talked a little beforehand to at least *pretend* that he had changed his mind, it wouldn't have been a big deal to me. It was just so tacky to bold-faced lie to avoid paying $6. I was so shocked I didn't know how to react initially. Obviously if I was just trying to ride a gravy train after hearing about his luxuries, I most certainly would have chosen a five-star restaurant and not a homely pizza joint. I was civil for the rest of the date. When I got home, I wrote him an email venting and blasting him for being a cheapskate. I never experienced anything like that again, thank goodness.

4 HAMMER TIME: RAYMOND

On a boring summer's day, I decided to reactivate my profile on a dating website. Although I generally did not entertain conversations with men without a single picture in their profile, I kind of enjoyed the mystery of Raymond. His profile was sparse, but the little that it had seemed okay. Soon, Raymond emailed me his picture. He claimed he wasn't very tech savvy and barely took pictures, so he only had one blurry picture from a few years back. He also didn't have a web cam, so I took a high risk of potentially being cat-fished. I wasn't looking for a boyfriend per se. I would be returning to London anyway, so I just wanted another adventure.

As we spoke on the phone, it was clear Raymond had some communication issues, not to mention he seemed to think the world was out to get him. He'd often cut me off in the middle of my sentences and didn't know how to disagree without being combative. I had to teach him some communication etiquette, such as not interrupting because it makes the other person feel like he is more concerned with getting his point across than actually understanding where the other person is coming from. I also told him that he projected a lot, and it would serve him better to be more objective and not interpret what the other person is saying according to how he would process the information, but rather in the context of that person's perspective. When in doubt, he could simply ask what they meant when they said something, rather than assuming what they meant or how they felt. This helped him tremendously with understanding how to be a more effective communicator (according to him).

When all of that was said and done, he wanted us to go to my favorite restaurant. In light of his blurry picture and my prior toothless date, I half jokingly asked if he had all 32 teeth. He said he only had 28, but I let him know 7 out of 8 ain't bad.

I took a bus and arrived at the mall, and I wasn't very impressed to say the least. His picture was more than a few years old, but he was respectful so I figured I would just be polite and sit through it. He was very fidgety, and seemed to be in a very negative space. He complained a lot about people and things, but I guess I opened Pandora's box when I assumed the position of a therapist.

He offered me a ride back home. Initially I wasn't very sure if I should take it, but I emailed his information to my best friend, and there were no red flags (thus far). I buckled my seat belt.

"Hang on a minute," he suddenly said. "I've gotta get something." He reached under his seat. I looked in his hand; he was waving a hammer.

OH MY GOD! I thought to myself. Please tell me this isn't my fate? Being bludgeoned to death with a hammer? By a guy I met online? What's wrong with me? I had watched enough Lifetime movies to know how these things can end. I leaned my body toward the door while opening the lock inconspicuously, ready to jump out the car if need be. "So ah, what do you plan to do with that?" I asked in a calm demeanor.

"Oh, I have to hit something in the hood of a car for it to start. I'll be right back!" he said as he got out the car.

I was so relieved. *So I'm not going to die after all.* But the ride itself had me thinking I may have spoken too soon.

First of all, his car was an old early 1990s jalopy, but the way he drove, you'd have thought it was a Ferrari. He had road rage like nobody's business, bobbing and weaving in and out of lanes, flipping people off, and rolling down the windows to revile the other drivers. "OH MY GOD! He's not going to *kill me*; he's going to *get us killed* talking to people like that and driving at these high speeds!" There are so many crazy people, as well as people on drugs, drunk, intemperate, impatient, and angry on the roads that I personally don't like to stir the pot. Maybe I've grown overly cautious, and my mom has rubbed off on me.

As soon as we arrived on my street, I thanked the heavens I made it home safely from this date with a loony. I didn't let him see my specific house, because I didn't fully trust his mental state. He asked me out on another date, but there was no way in hell I'd do that again. I'm just happy I made it out alive, and that I didn't end up on the news following that date!

5 WHAT'S MY NAME? STANLEY

On a rainy London evening, I was bored so I decided to peruse through Craigslist. In New York, Craigslist was notorious for booty calls and potential serial killers, but I wanted to test this new market. I put up a regular dating ad since I was new in town. While browsing through the plethora of responses, one in particular caught my eye. A certain gentleman named Stanley had a decent enough picture, and it seemed as though we had enough in common to meet up.

I decided on this phenomenal Thai spot in my neck of the woods that served decadent, authentic cuisine with a low-key atmosphere—perfect for a no frills first date. On top of that, it was one of my favorite hidden gems in London. When we met, we had a great time on our first date. He was pretty funny, and I made fun of him relentlessly for talking about himself in the third person. I had never met anyone quite like him. Throughout the night, I referred to him as "Stanley" and his email address also contained that name, so nothing seemed out of the ordinary.

Without fail, every time I called him, he would answer the phone. Until one night, he missed my call. It went to voicemail. Much to my surprise, although it was obviously his voice, the message said, "Hi, you've reached the voicemail of Jason. I can't get to the phone right now so leave your name, number, and a brief message, and I will get back to you as soon as possible." I was a bit perplexed so I just hung up the phone. He called me back promptly, and I couldn't help but to belt out, "Who are you? Why are you lying about your name? This is borderline creepy!"

"My real name is Jason," he replied. "As a working professional, I didn't feel comfortable giving out my real name to a stranger from Craigslist until I actually got to know the person. I'm sorry."

I paused for about 10 seconds to process what had just taken place.

"Don't you think the moment we met and you saw I was normal that that was the time to reveal the truth?" I asked. "Why would you let me call you Stanley all night for not one, but two dates and never correct me? If I didn't call and get your voicemail, were you just going to continue in that lie?"

He assured me I was making a bigger deal of it than it really was, and eventually I tried to empathize with him, as I knew the Internet could be a dangerous place. I myself was pretty cautious.

About two dates later, another surprise surfaced from the woodwork. We exchanged Skype usernames, and then I went to his profile (I think subconsciously I had issues fully trusting his word after the previous lie) and lo and behold, he had another name yet again. I promptly told him that he was freaking me out and anyone who conceals his identity to that capacity without being a celebrity, in a witness protection program, or a secret agent has something fishy to hide. I didn't want to potentially deal with bigger bombs in the future. He told me the name on his Skype account was his real name in his native language. There wasn't enough invested to pursue something serious with him, so I let our romance fall by the wayside.

6 THE YOUNG & THE HOPELESS: BRIAN

In my late teens I met a smart, funny, and witty man who was five years my senior. His name was Brian. To date, he is one of the most intelligent and unbelievable people I've ever met and probably will ever meet. It all started with hotornot.com. With a mutual vote for the other being hot, a conversation then ensued. It didn't matter to us that we were across the country from each other; nor did we, at the time, try to work out the logistics. All we knew was that we would have long and fulfilling conversations all the time on the phone. Truth be told, I never even fathomed we would ever really meet.

Brain sort of had a messed-up childhood that unfortunately pushed him to generally have lower standards. We eventually entertained the idea of dating, but I was a bit hesitant because of our conflicting spiritual beliefs, and there was no way I'd ever move to Minnesota. I already had my career goals, and there were only a few cities in which I could really flourish. He ran a very successful contracting business. By 15, he had graduated high school, and by 18, he had started a successful construction business that afforded him a great lifestyle. As a highly ambitious person myself, he truly inspired me. I learned so much from him because he was just one of those people who you'd want to hang around and be motivated. He was so well-spoken and didn't mind a good challenge.

After about two years of a phone friendship, he decided to fly to my state to see me for the first time. I was very nervous but I was confident that if something weren't right, it would be evident within that time frame. Despite my reservations, we had a blast, and he was my best kiss. We cruised through the city in my little hybrid car, singing our favorite pop songs, caressing each other, and enjoying the company.

He decided to take another trip to see me six weeks later, and once again, it was magical. He told me he was willing to move to be with me, but I didn't take him seriously enough to make the poor chap jump ship all the way across the country. I had plans to leave the state anyway. I told him we should take it slow.

Somehow, I have this uncanny ability to make people (men especially) feel so much at ease that they divulge information that they should really save for one of their male friends and not a woman they're pursuing. He nonchalantly told me about two women he had slept with since our meet-up. Apparently, he lost his virginity to one of them, and both of them were "selfish lovers." We weren't official, and we never really went that far physically, so I wasn't exactly irate but rather disappointed. I figured he didn't really take our situation as seriously as I had originally thought. Furthermore, when Brian and I met up, it was during the interim of my initial break-up with my first love and our imminent reconciliation. I was not prepared for his reaction to the news.

He bawled hysterically on the phone. "But I'm in love with you. How could you do this to me? This isn't fair!" I didn't know whether to laugh or to empathize. I couldn't believe he thought it was okay to sleep with other people and expect me to simply twiddle my thumbs…but that's not even the craziest part!

He tried for a while to get me back, but I was adamant about sticking it out with my first love. We maintained a friendship (after all, that was our foundation anyway), and I was flabbergasted by his next choice of lady. He met some girl online and on their first date, a guy smashed his head with a bottle. That guy happened to be her alleged "ex" boyfriend. Brian ended up getting several stitches. You would think that would ring the alarm and signal the death knell of that romance, but no. He decided to continue to see her. I asked him if he was sure that her ex was really in the past, because it seemed pretty illogical for someone to behave in such a manner unless they felt betrayed and/or have mental/emotional issues. There was no restraining order against him, so I wondered if Brian was the rebound and this girl was playing them both. Nevertheless, against his better judgment, he continued seeing her.

She lived with him for a while, and one day he went home to find her gone. He drove through the whole town, knocking on doors in a desperate attempt to find her. Eventually he did find her with another man, and he wasn't the violent ex-boyfriend either. He begged her to come back and so she did. No less than a month later, she disappeared again. This time, she told him she was pregnant and wasn't sure who was the father. At first, he said he wanted a DNA test to determine the paternity of the child. Then he said he loved her too much and didn't care, and he ran off and married her. He assumed full responsibility for the child and had to tell his religious organization what he had done. He was excommunicated for six months and couldn't even speak to his own mother. Ridiculous on many levels to most, but I respected his beliefs. His solution was marriage. His stepfather cheated on his mom for over 15 years, and he eventually changed.

That said, Brian figured there was hope for his girlfriend as well.

She was the jealous type, so after he told me about his marriage plans, he said we couldn't talk anymore and I respected that. I still miss our conversations and the fun we had from time to time, but such is life.

7 MR. CHICKEN WING: XAVIER

After years of hearing all the hype and watching the incessant commercials, I decided to give eHarmony a stab. I was so over the free sites and the lack of quality within them, so I paid for one of the most renowned dating sites in the world.

Xavier was perhaps one of the youngest people I had gone on a date with at the time; he and I were the same age (23). We had a date planned, and I was pretty excited about it. He seemed to have a good head on his shoulders with a lot of things going for him. The only thing that kind of alarmed me a little was that he had no male figure in his life—just two sisters and his mother. That may or may not have played a part in his behavior, but it left an indelible mark, and he would eventually go down in history as one of the pettiest people I've ever dated.

We scheduled a movie date for 9 o'clock, as I would finish my finance class at 8. He got off on time, but had some engagements prior to our date. I matter of factly mentioned how after a long day, I just knew I was going to be starving.

"Oh, then you should probably grab something to eat," he said.

I decided to go into this chicken shack by the theatre, as I didn't want to be on edge due to hunger, especially after a 12-hour school day. I received a call from him, stating he had arrived about five minutes after I began eating my food. I asked him if I could just finish eating really quick because if the movie theatres were like those in America, I could not bring outside food in there.

"Just put it in your purse, it shouldn't be a big deal," he said.

I promptly did as he suggested. I got there by tube and he by car, so he had to park. I went to the back of the theatre to the parking lot, but it was busy and I couldn't spot him, so I phoned him.

"I don't see you, Xavier. Where are you?"

"I see you! Turn to the left, no to the right, no, you're close, awww no, a little more to the left," he directed me.

"This isn't working. Can you at least stick your hand out the window and wave so I know where you are?"

"It's too cold!"

"Seriously, Xavier? Man up and stop being lazy! You know what, just park and meet me at the door."

We finally met up, and he asked me if I wanted some popcorn.

"Sure, why not?"

"Well, I only eat sweet popcorn."

"I only eat salty," I told him.

"No salty, I'm getting sweet. Trust me, it's good."

"You can get a bucket of sweet popcorn if you'd like, but you asked me what I wanted, and I told you I don't eat sweet."

He went ahead and got sweet popcorn anyway. We sat down in the theatre.

"Why aren't you eating the popcorn?" he asked, clearly frustrated.

"I told you about umpteen times I DO NOT eat sweet popcorn, and you insisted. Eat to your heart's content."
He then asked me for one of my chicken wings. I must

admit, I have always been the type of girl who would rather buy someone else what I am eating than to share it. It's just how it is. As a person whose face speaks before her lips, I'm almost certain I had a "you've got to be kidding me" facial expression.

He drove me home, and it was very silent. That same night he decided to call me to deliver feedback from our date.

"You looked pretty upset when I asked you for a chicken wing, I cannot believe it! You are selfish!"

"Dude, you TOLD ME if I was hungry, I should get something to eat. I figured you would follow your own advice too! Is that so unreasonable? Furthermore, when you came, I was in a restaurant! How hard would it have been to just say, 'Hey, I didn't get a chance to get something to eat. Can you grab me something too?' I would have happily done so! I'm not a mind reader, so don't expect telepathy. You seem very stubborn, impractical, petty, and childish; I have no time for it. Good-bye!"

I don't remember his exact rebuttal, but I do remember it being so insulting that I vowed to never speak to him again, and I felt inclined to tell him to grow a pair. About a year later, I received a text from him telling me how much he missed me.

"Dude, you argued with me over popcorn and A CHICKEN WING," I said. "Think about it, A. CHICKEN. WING! How old are we? You bought something I told you from the get go I do not eat, anyway, and then got mad at me for not eating it. On top of that, you had the nerve to insult me. Let's be realistic here. Neither one of us were thinking about the other that much, as a whole year has passed and we haven't even said a word to each other. You have been doing just fine, and I will continue to be fine as well, *without* you. All the best!"

8 THE YOUNG & THE FLATULENT: SKYLAR

Skylar and I seemed to have a great vibe from the moment we met online. We chatted for over a year before we'd actually meet in person. (This was before Tinder, and today's notion to meet up ASAP.) We both had a great sense of humor, so we found ourselves cracking up in every conversation we ever had. One day, we decided to take it to the next level and meet in real life. I was pretty enthusiastic about it, and the place of choice was the movies. I don't recall the exact movie, but I remember having so much fun...until a minor interruption.

"Do you smell that? Whoa, that's offensive!" he belted as he let out a huge chuckle.

"Wow. REAL mature!" I thought to myself as the stench permeated the air. Honestly speaking, it ruined it for me. I couldn't believe this man who seemed respectable and down to earth would do something like this, especially on a first date. It would have been one thing if he at least had the decency to excuse himself, but to lay one on me without warning rubbed me the wrong way.

First impressions count. I automatically marked him off

my list; if he couldn't even hold it together on a first date when you should present your best self, imagine how he might lack tact in other situations—it wasn't worth the risk. The once giddy and upbeat girl became slightly withdrawn and quiet; since we were watching a movie, it didn't warrant any suspicion. I thought he would just let it go, but he didn't.

"Can you believe that in the movie theatre? That was a pretty intense fart," he said.

"Excuse me? It's super rude to pass gas and then continuously harp on it, as if my nose wasn't already offended enough!"

"Oh, that wasn't me!" he said while still laughing.

I didn't believe him. He was a pretty devout man; still yet, he wasn't prepared for my next move. "I don't believe you, and I have a small Bible in my purse," I said. "Put your hand on this Bible and say you didn't fart in the movie theatre if you're telling me the truth."

He put his hand on the Bible. "I didn't do it."

"Nuh-uh, say it in full. 'I, Skylar Smith, did not fart in the movie theatre.'"

He repeated after me. "I, Skylar Smith, did not fart in the movie theatre." I believed him then. We both laughed hysterically as we strolled along the parking lot for 20 minutes. I was just as shocked at my maneuver as he. I couldn't believe I had gotten someone to take on oath, on a Bible at that, that they did not fart in a theatre. Though it didn't pan out romantically for other reasons, we're still good friends. From time to time, we still laugh about one of our most memorable first dates.

9 THE MARRIAGE BROKER: COREY

While perusing the aisles of the department store Daffy's, I noticed a well-dressed guy staring at me. He was in the company of a friend, and we exchanged looks back and forth, but that was all. I made my way down to the second floor, and there I saw him again. Eventually, he came up to me and struck up a conversation.

"Hi, my name is Corey. I noticed you from the previous floor and figured the least I could do was say hello," he said in introduction. We started talking and exchanged numbers, but it would be some weeks before we would hang out for the first time. Although Corey was forward in his approach, he was never pushy afterward, which was refreshing and unlike many of the men I had encountered in New York. He had just moved from Albania, and was probably one of the sweetest people (to a fault) I had ever met. We went to a nice French restaurant, Chez Josephine, followed by a movie.

Afterward, he revealed his initial hesitation with American women. When he first moved to New York, he met a lady, asked her on a date and waited four hours for her to show up, but she never did. I admired his patience because I'd go out on a limb to say at least 90 percent of

25

New Yorkers wouldn't have had that kind of patience. He also told me that he had recently met a hot girl at a club, took her home, and when they were about to get it on, she revealed she was a transsexual. He said he had never heard of this before, so he asked her what that meant. After she explained, he said he hit the ground running—literally—from his own apartment, screaming up and down the street. I think he most likely kissed her first, and then she revealed it. He claims he never kissed her, but I didn't believe him. It didn't matter anyway.

We'd hang out here and there, and he was always a great gentleman. He never really tried to put any "moves" on me, and I played it safe by not assuming he had romantic intentions. We taught each other a lot about our respective cultures. It was the random call one day that had me thinking he couldn't really be that naïve.

"Hey, I really need to talk to you about business. You seem like a trustworthy person, and I'd like to share this venture with you. I'll buy you lunch, and we can discuss it."

"Okay," I replied. "What kind of business? What is this about?"

"Don't worry, I will tell you everything in person. You might really love this idea. Let's meet at Bryant Park around noon."

We had talked about my entrepreneurial ambitions in our many chats before, so I thought for sure that he had some kind of legit business to discuss. I had to hold in my laughter as he proposed this ridiculous scenario.

"So here's what I want to talk to you about. I have this friend – he wants to live in America. He's pretty well to do back home in Albania, and he wants to come here. He met a guy who is willing to marry him; he's totally straight, but it's strictly for papers. He'd prefer a woman. He will put you up in one of these apartments in Bryant Park for a year and then pay you $10,000 at the end of that year when he comes, and you will live together. He needs a new webcam and has to use an Internet café so he cannot Skype with you at the moment, but you can exchange emails and start to develop a rapport."

What on earth I could have ever said to make him think I was so hungry for money that I would jeopardize my freedom for a mere $10,000 was beyond my comprehension, but then again, I am just being logical. "Wait a minute, are you being for real, or is this a joke?" I asked. I obviously knew he was being serious, or he wouldn't have gone through buying me lunch, but sometimes it helps to say what you're thinking out loud.

"What? He found a guy? Gay marriage isn't even legal in New York yet; domestic partnership is limited to just visits but not a permanent stay, and you know by protocol he has to have pictures kissing and know intimate details about his partner, don't you? You can't just sashay in the office thinking they're not going to ask you personal questions and ask to see evidence that proves you are together. This isn't their first rodeo!" I told him.

"Come on! $10,000 and year of living in Bryant Park! That's a sweet deal."

"Look, my parents are still together and I take marriage VERY seriously. This also goes against my spiritual beliefs and rudimentary ethics. Do you know the amount of jail time I could serve for this? For a meager $10,000? And what kind of idiot would I be if I didn't request at least half the cash up front? No way!"

I also thought about other practical things (e.g., if he changed his mind at any point, I'd be stuck with an expensive apartment that was in my name, ruining my credit). Furthermore, if this guy was well off (even by his country's standards), how could he not have Internet at home, let alone a simple, an inexpensive webcam? A sucker is born every minute, but I surely was not one of them. He eventually relented and faded into obscurity, but overall, he was one of the most interesting people I have ever met.

10 SUPERMAN COMPLEX: ADAM

When Adam and I began corresponding, it was shortly after seeing each for the second time on another dating website. We couldn't communicate on the first site since I was a non-paying member. That said, I thought it was nothing short of fate when we were finally able to chat. Although I generally prefer dark hair and olive skin, something about Adam stood out. He was about 6'5" with blonde hair and striking blue eyes. He also had a very masculine, athletic physique, which I loved. I struck up the first conversation we had.

"You know, this might sound funny but I've seen you before on another website, but I wasn't able to contact you then. How are you doing?" I asked. That was the inception of our romance. We exchanged numbers and emailed back and forth for about a week before finally meeting in person.

It was a beautiful summer night in the Big Apple. We first went to dinner at this Thai place he had raved about, and afterward we strolled along Bryant Park and had great conversation. That is, until he started talking about his mother in a negative light. Experience has taught me that men with mommy issues are usually not the best partners.

He later explained the issues she was battling, and then I felt more empathetic toward him.

"You know, sometimes I just wish someone would try to push my date onto the train tracks so I could save her," he said as we waited for the train.

"What? Is that some kind of tasteless joke?" I asked, as I slowly maneuvered my way to the middle of the platform, playing it safe.

"I'm telling you, most men have a superhero complex. They want to rescue a woman and feel strong and like a hero."

"Well, I'll be perfectly honest with you...you sound completely off your rocker, and I suggest refraining from telling any other woman that philosophy, on the first date, or *ever*. I have never heard anything remotely like it in my life. Any funny moves while we are here wise guy, and I will give you a certified butt whooping. Look at me! Look into my eyes!" I stared intently, motioning my eyes to his with my index and middle finger. "I am very serious! No one will push me onto any tracks! Got it?"

"It obviously wouldn't be *me* pushing the date; how else would I save her?" I never heard anything like it before, but otherwise and overall he seemed like an okay person, and I took my standard precautionary measures of emailing my best friend the picture, name, email, phone number, occupation, and planned date when going out with any new man. We continued to hang out, and eventually we became really good friends.

11 MR. LOVE YOU LONG TIME: MICHAEL

While I was no stranger to online and conventional dating, I had never tried speed dating. I figured it could be a wonderful new experience. I had no clue what to expect, but I decided to play it by ear. If nothing else, it would be a good excuse to get pretty and mingle in my new city (London). All of my single girlfriends in grad school were eager for me to give a review of the experience.

I entered the local restaurant/pub in a dazzling cream lace and jersey dress, a full face of make-up, thick eyelashes, and a nice high bun. I hardly wear anything besides lip gloss and eyeliner, but this was a special occasion. I was a bit skeptical of the event, since there were far more open spots left for men than women; I knew there'd be about three women to one man, and the competition would be fierce. As we sipped wine and waited on the host to announce when the event would officially begin, I tried to see if there would be anyone I could possibly connect with. There were about three gentlemen out of that bunch that I found relatively attractive.

I finally got to sit with one of the guys I had found most attractive. His approach was much too stiff, and it felt like an interview. Almost as if I was applying for a job to be his girlfriend—no thanks!

There was a fourth gentleman who was average looking, but we seemed to have the best conversation. Maybe it was because he was liquored up, but he seemed pretty easygoing. After the event was over, we went to the bar section of the restaurant and ordered some drinks. We then exchanged numbers and made plans for a future date. It seemed simple enough.

We went to a restaurant called Jaime's and ordered relatively decent food on our first date. He then took me to his waterfront apartment in Canary Wharf, as he was an investment banker. We seemed to have decent enough conversation, but one of the things I've learned is to never trust people who harp too much about money when it is irrelevant at that particular stage or situation. He began to tell me about his beautiful African ex-girlfriend, who expected the world of him, including funding her living expenses. I didn't ask him anything pertaining to his former flames, let alone their financial arrangement. He lamented over the things he had to buy her.

We then planned a second formal date at a church. I had never gone on a date in church, but as strange as it sounded, I thought why not? When I saw him outside of his suit and tie (during speed dating and our first date, he was dressed up), he wore high-water jeans that were unraveling at the hem—a bit ironic considering that usually happens when pants that are too long drag on the ground. Anyway, we chit-chatted for over a week on the phone. It was by the end of the second week, I figured out he had many, many issues.

"I want to know where is this going?" he asked. Apparently in the British culture (and arguably Europe in general), people move into relationships a lot faster than most of us Americans do. Americans will sometimes "talk to" or "hang out" with someone for months without putting an official title on it.

"I mean, we are getting to know each other, aren't we?" I asked. "It's too soon for me to commit to anything, if that's what you're asking. We've only been out twice."

"What? Have you no heart, woman? Here I am falling in love with you, and you're telling me you're just trying to 'figure it out!' You should be falling in love too! What's there to figure out? You are one cold, heartless person; yes, that's what you are! I have invested all this time and energy, and you don't love me? Really? Well, now you owe me a dinner! You need to tell me the time and place you are going to take me out because you have to pay me back!"

I laughed for a few minutes straight. *Oh these Brits and their sense of humor! Good one!* I then tried to change the subject, but he started to hurl low-key insults at me, the way clever Brits know how to do. I really didn't want to have to take it there and told him my credentials proved I am far from "thick." I told him not to ever call or text me again, and I promptly hung up the phone. The funny part is after that, he constantly tried to add me on all social media profiles. He even had the gall to write me an email about six months later about reconciliation, as if there was anything left to be reconciled in the first place. That nipped future speed-dating considerations in the bud for me.

.

12 THE ENTREPRENEURIAL ARTIST: THOMAS

On a cold winter day, I hastily hopped on a bus. I was pretty much minding my own business, trying to ensure I didn't miss my stop as I was still familiarizing myself with London. About half-way through the ride, I struck up a conversation with a gentleman asking for directions. We ended up talking for an extended amount of time, and I asked him what he did; it complemented what I was doing as well, so I suggested exchanging emails.

Our conversations were strictly about business for the first couple months. As I got to know him, I was completely blown away by his energy and his ability to be both artistic and business minded; anyone who is familiar with both types of people know how much of an anomaly it is to find an artist whose artistic passion doesn't impede his ability to be a bit more practical on the business side of things. I considered myself of the same mindset, so I found this quality refreshing. He was also a go-getter. If he said he was going to take pictures of the Royals at their next soiree, that's exactly what he would do. We all know people who have very lofty goals but never actually follow through. He actually walked his talk, and that increased my admiration.

One day he asked me to accompany him to Ikea to help him choose some furniture. I had never been to Ikea in Europe, so I joined him in this venture. It was in that instance that it became clear he had a romantic interest in me, so we began to know each other on a different level; the dynamic of our relationship changed, which isn't always a good thing.

For our first date, he took me to this heavenly Ethiopian place for my birthday, and we had a blast. We took lots of pictures and exchanged our first kiss.

"Hey, my mom lives right there. Let's go pay her a visit," he said on our way back to the tube. I initially thought he was being facetious, but by his demeanor, I realized he was being very serious. I politely declined, and he was quite upset about it. I just personally found that to be too much too soon, especially at that time of night. I didn't want that kind of pressure. From a cultural and personal perspective, meeting parents is completely out of the question unless it's a serious relationship. It was our *first* date! I had on a sexy number (albeit classy), and his mom being a preacher (although he himself was not religious at all) would make it even more awkward and uncomfortable for me. I wasn't sure how she would receive me, and I didn't want to take that risk. Regardless of her occupation, I'd want to be dressed modestly the first time I meet parents. This was one of the ornaments that he would hold over my head begrudgingly for the rest of our relationship.

We continued to see each other, and we had a tumultuous (emotionally speaking) relationship. As he endowed me with his professional wisdom, I asked what could I offer him in exchange because I didn't think it would be fair to be the only one gaining some kind of benefit. He then asked me to teach him how to love. From the beginning, he had told me his issues with receiving love and being emotionally open with women; that inability contributed a lot to his previous relationships' demises. I don't know why I still chose to see him. Perhaps it was the fascination of his mind and how it worked. Maybe it was how amazing he was at what he did, so I was in awe of him. We would butt heads often because we were both strong-willed people; he was determined to not have any form of confrontation so no issues would ever truly be addressed—yet I was very confrontational and wanted to discuss and resolve issues. He would disappear for days at a time. Sometimes we'd just run into each other spontaneously, as he lived right up the street. I also found out via Skype after curiously checking his profile a few months into things that he was four years older than he said he was. What I thought was a man only 10 years my senior turned out to be 14!

What amazed me the most was his reaction to my moving to New York to complete my thesis. He sobbed as I broke the news to him, and that made really think that I meant something to him. To be fair, I didn't allow myself to fall for him emotionally, but I had a lot of love for him as an individual.

During our last meeting, he looked at me with tears in his eyes. "You're not coming back, are you?" he asked.

"Well I *have to* come back for graduation and to present my thesis, so yes, I will. I even want to try to get a job out here," I replied. We never really spoke of expectations when I was leaving.

Within a short period of time, I discovered that the man who had been crying a couple weeks prior, as if he was deeply in love and saddened by my absence, found my replacement very quickly. I wasn't exactly upset with him; I was just taken aback that after five months of dating and looking teary eyed just before I left, it happened so soon. Evidently, his "devastation" didn't last very long, and he was the one telling me how quickly he knew I'd move on in New York. I wanted to find out diplomatically what was going on to confirm and affirm my intuition from his Facebook posts.

There was one lady in particular that I found a bit suspicious. She was a dancer, and one of his photography clients. I suppose that was a downside to dating a photographer; always meeting different women. That coupled with his intelligence, connections, charismatic personality, and looks meant women threw themselves at him regularly. She was Polish and wrote something in her native tongue that I translated via Google. She was calling him endearing terms that didn't seem to reflect a strictly platonic or professional relationship. I just had a bad vibe about it, so I felt out the situation.

"Greetings and kisses from New York," I wrote on his Facebook page. I knew if he were seeing her, she'd be curious (at the very least) as to who I was. I also wanted to make it innocent enough to not appear obvious and to prevent possibly being deleted from his Facebook friends before reading more about their interactions on his page.

One day, she was feeling nostalgic so she wrote: "Remember that night, listening to Otis Redding's 'These Arms of Mine,' sipping on tea and having that discussion?" I commented just to mess around with her head a bit: "Yea, I know! Oh my gosh, that song is just way too amazing! A classic for sure." She then emailed me shortly after: "Hey, I see that you're a friend of Thomas and from New York; do you live there? I'm moving to New York. Can you tell me some cool spots to check out?" I just replied: "I have no clue who you are! Google is your best friend. Have a great day!" By far, this is one of the bitchiest things I have ever done, but his lack of being straightforward led me to find an alternative way to get the truth. He was still contacting me while I was in New York and telling me how much he missed me, though he failed to mention a new person in his life. I asked him who she was and why she was using so many terms of endearment towards him. He told me she was only one of his clients and that's it. I pressed him for the truth on several more occasions until he finally confessed they had been seeing each other, but it was nothing serious. I then told him he needed to tell her not to contact me. Long story short, I cut him off and deleted him from everything. He eventually apologized and we saw each other a few times when I moved back to London. I decided it was a dead end romantically speaking, and we lost touch.

13 MEET MY WIFE: WILLIAM

After my dating hiatus was up, I decided to put myself out there again on Plenty of Fish (also known as Plenty of Shit). I actually had some level of success on it a couple years prior and figured at the very least, I could forge new friendships. Then along came William. We had been exchanging emails here and there for a while when he finally asked for my number.

He called me much more than I called him, and at one point, he even threatened to stop contacting me when he didn't feel I initiated communication enough. I let him know school was my number one priority, and I was busting my chops to make sure I graduated at the top of my class, so if that was problematic, then he should do what he felt was best. He apologized for not understanding, and we planned our first date.

He came to the restaurant almost one hour late. I was trying to be more easygoing than I'd been in the past, so I let it slide. One thing I did love about William was that he was probably one of the best conversationalists I've ever met. We could talk about politics, philosophy, current events, etc. for hours on end and never tire. He appreciated my sass, delivery of my stories, and the way I articulated things.

We dated for about eight months, often breaking up and then getting back together. He would do something stupid or insensitive, I would ignore him; he would plead, and then I would take him back. Lather, rinse, repeat. About seven months into things, he revealed that he was married after I caught him in a half-truth. I was shocked because I'd often spend days at a time over at his place; we'd go out until the wee hours of the morning, and we'd talk very late at night.

"WHAT! You wait seven months to tell me this? What's wrong with you?"

"Well, truth is, I only married her for papers. She lives in Canada now and has a child by another man—a white man. She is also Kenyan, but got her British papers and we met while in uni. I have to pay her every month until I get my citizenship."

"Do you have any children?

"No, we never had any children. It was strictly business."

I also found out via Skype that he was three years older than he claimed.

"Nobody tells the truth in their online dating profiles. You have to embellish a little," he said.

"Well I tell the truth in my profiles! I had no idea honesty was so passé," I quipped.

Things got a bit rocky, but boredom got the best of me. I wasn't open to meeting anyone new (was tired of the dating process), so I continued going out with him for several more weeks. One night, we had already planned a date so I called him to confirm.

"Hey, so we're meeting at 9 right?"

"Well, my good friend from Canada is in town, and she's having a party and invited me."

"Oh, well if she's here all the way from Canada, we could always reschedule. It's totally fine. Have fun!"

"Well actually, I am sure she would love to meet you.

Would you like to come?"

"Ehh…I'm not really in the mood to party tonight. Honestly, have a blast and we'll catch up later!"

"No, I insist. She'd be upset if she knew my girlfriend was around, and she didn't get to meet her."

"Okay," I said. "I'll be ready in about an hour."

"All right, see you then!"

When he came to pick me up, there were two women and a baby in the back seat of his car. He didn't tell me there'd already be people in the car, so it was a bit strange. We soon arrived at the woman with the baby's place, and it was just the five of us including the baby.

That's odd, I thought to myself. *How is this a party if only the five of us are here?* "Are other people coming?" I asked.

"I'm not sure," the woman with the baby said.

She then offered me some food she'd made, and I was hungry to my core, but by the way it smelled and looked, I had to pass. My face would definitely speak before my lips, and if it wasn't good, I wasn't going to eat it, so I played it safe. He ate the food and commented on how it was yummy, but I wasn't buying it. Nadia, the woman with the child, then asked me to take photos with her son. He was mixed race and so adorable.

"Sure!" I said as I handed her my phone to take the pictures. I then went on to change his diaper and cuddle with the adorable tot.

The next step was the interrogation, and that's when I grew suspicious. I didn't want to be rude to William's friends, but they began speaking in their native tongue, which is really impolite and inconsiderate. Then Nadia and her homely sidekick decided to ask me 21 questions, as if I were on trial. They bombarded me with probing questions: "So how did you guys meet? How long have you known each other? How long have you been dating? Do you really like him? You'd better treat our friend right!" Nadia even pointed to her child and said, "In a year or so, I want to see one of these running around." They looked me up and down, observing every curve and detail. I tried to answer the questions I deemed appropriate.

"Do you want a drink?" they asked.

"No, I am okay," I replied.

William then chimed in. "Honey, I'll make you a drink."

I was counting down the minutes until the night was over. I felt weird and uncomfortable. On the drive home, I had to sock it to William.

"What the hell was that about, William?"

"What, honey?"

"Why were your 'friends' interrogating me? Why were they being so intrusive? It was beyond the normal questions one would ask when first meeting someone. Telling me I'd better have a child running around in a year. Is she mad?"

"Don't pay it any mind, honey. You know women; they ask a lot of questions and we've known each other for a long time, so of course she's just trying to look out for me."

I dropped the subject. The next day, while in the shower, revelation hit me like a ton of bricks and I began to reason within myself. *Wait a minute*! His friend's name is Nadia, but his wife's name is Nadeng. Nadia has a mixed race child about the same age and lives in Canada, but so does Nadeng. *No, no, it could not be! He would never have the cojones to lie to me and set me up like that…would he? Maybe this is all in my head.* In my heart of hearts, I knew what was up so I called him fuming.

"William, are you out of your freaking mind?! That was not your friend from Canada William, but your WIFE! Your freaking wife! Why on earth would you bring her to my residence? She could be crazy for all I know! Why would you lie to me like that? What's wrong with you? No wonder she was grilling me like that! She just wanted to size me up. She and her facially challenged accomplice! How dare you!"

"Look, honey. She has me by the balls, okay? I have to do everything she says because she holds the key to my citizenship! She overheard our conversation, and when she is in town I have to be her chauffeur and essentially her bitch. She insisted that she wanted to meet you."

"I don't want to hear it! I have no idea about the conversations the two of you have let alone what you are or are not promising her. I can't believe you brought her to my residence on top of being married in the first place! Suppose you tick her off and she decides to pop in and start trouble? This is entirely inappropriate. I don't know what kind of circus you guys are running, but I want NO part of it. This is the final straw! Good-bye!"

William continually tried contacting me for over a year. Every time I ignored him; he was an opportunist and dishonest person to the maximum level. In the past, I've had to deal with a crazy ex-girlfriend who got my family's address and phone numbers, and threatened me, so I don't like to take certain chances. What if he told her they would get back together, and she never knew he was seeing someone? He didn't seem to have an honest bone in his body, and my life was too valuable to risk. Sometimes I do miss our conversations but overall, I was happy to get away from the drama and deception that came with that package.

14 THE VIRTUAL CASANOVA: JEREMIAH

Within a week of putting a profile back up on Plenty of Fish after my year hiatus, I met Jeremiah. He wasn't exactly a man of many words, but we had some common interests. We spoke for about a week or two before we met up. He wanted our first date to be at his place, but there was no way in hell I was going to go to a stranger's house in a foreign country. So we agreed to meet at a pub up the street from my house. I normally wouldn't go on such a late first date, but since I lived up the street, I agreed to meet him at 10:30 after he got off work.

We sat down for about an hour and a half, and he bought me a drink. It was a weekday so the pub was closing within 30 minutes.

"Man, I'm really enjoying our conversation," he said.

"Let's go back my house."

"For what?"

"So we can talk."

"Wow, you must really think I'm simple. I am not going over some random man's house at this hour of the night to 'talk.' You live an hour away and trains stop running by 1:30, so I'd be stuck over there. I know what you've got up your sleeve, and I'm afraid it ain't happening, buddy."

I couldn't believe he'd think I'd place such little value on myself that after a single drink and first time meeting, I'd be ready to go to bed with him.

"Oh, no no no!" he said. "It's not like that. I have an extra room. I wasn't insinuating anything."

"Well, you have two options: talk to me here until this place closes or talk to me on THE PHONE for as long as your little heart desires because I am going back home."

"Can I walk you to your house?"

"Nope, but I can walk you to the train station."

"Okay."

As we walked toward the station about five minutes away, this handsome young man approached us. Unfortunately, this man had drinking problems, and it made me a little sad.

"Hey there guys!" the man said.

"Hello!" we replied.

He then started to have small talk with us, and revealed he was from Sierra Leone. My date was from Ghana, and he told him no wonder he was so handsome; Sierra Leoneans are known to be handsome. It was a little strange to see him compliment the man like that, but I barely knew anything about the African culture so I figured it must be the norm.

"Wow, she's gorgeous!" he said. "You should take my number! Just kidding, ha ha!" the young man said, as he bobbed from side to side in a semi-stupor.

"Hey, hey, hey! You are trespassing!" Jeremiah said as his demeanor did a complete 180. There was slight anger in his eyes. "Come on, honey. Let's go."

I laughed until tears ran down my face. I found the whole situation and conversation hilarious.

After that, Jeremiah suggested we had a real date since during drinks we'd got on well. Between my school schedule and his work schedule, it was a bit tricky planning another date, but he told me about a French restaurant he knew that I would like. We planned to go the following Friday.

I got all dressed up and called him to confirm when he wasn't answering his phone. Was this guy for real?

The next day, he called me, apologizing profusely that he had to work overtime and couldn't get around to calling me. He was punctual for our first date and didn't give me any reason to question him up until that point, so I gave him the benefit of the doubt. About a month would go by before I'd hear from him again.

"Hey, I've been so busy, sorry."

"Okay…"

"Let's go to that French restaurant, okay?"

"If you say so," I said. "But how about this? You call me an hour and a half before, on the day of, and then I'll believe you."

"Okay. I am so sorry."

"Look, I'm about to walk into this job interview so we can't talk now."

"Okay, I will call you later."

The day came and, of course, I never heard from him again. I started perusing through the site again and lo and behold, he had not one, but TWO different profiles on the SAME website. His name was different and the content of the profile was almost the same and the picture was the same. I figured he was running some kind of scheme, so I wrote him an email on the second profile.

"Dude, what the hell! Why do you have two different profiles on the same site with the same picture? What kind of game are you running here?"

"Look, the ladies like to see that you're not daft, so you have to change it up a bit."

"No, this seems like you're running some kind of scheme or game."

"No, I am not."

45

A week later, (God as my witness) I saw a THIRD profile with a different name; this time he used a different picture. I decided I would ignore his calls from then on because clearly he was unreliable and most likely preying on poor, innocent women on these dating sites.

Almost two months went by without a peep from him. One night he called, and I rejected it. He then sent me a text he had been robbed and because I do have a heart, I decided to call him to make sure he was okay.

"Oh my God, you were robbed? Are you okay? Was it at gunpoint? Where did it happen? How did it happen? Did the police catch him?"

"No, it was a woman who robbed me."

"A *woman*?"

"Yes."

"How did this happen?"

"Well about a couple months ago, I met this girl online and I told her to come over for our first date and I would cook for her. We had a great time. She then would come over sometimes. I'd cook, and we'd hang out. I even let her borrow £300 the second week we met."

"So let me get this straight: the REAL reason you were standing me up all this time was because you were seeing someone? And you have the cheek to tell me this same woman robbed you?"

"I know, I'm sorry! I just never thought she would rob me!"

"What did she steal?"

"Well I left my wallet on the table when I used the bathroom. She stayed the whole weekend, and I didn't notice anything. It wasn't until the day after she left I noticed £400 missing and two of my credit cards."

"Well did you file a police report?"

"No, I guess I should, huh?"

"DUH! And cancel the credit cards. Wow, she must have really put it on for you, an otherwise intelligent engineer to lose all of your damn senses. What were you thinking lending £300 to someone you barely knew? And furthermore, why in the world would you leave your wallet around a complete stranger? Must have been the best you've ever had."

"Uh, we didn't have sex."

"Seriously, Jeremiah? You *still* haven't learned, have you? Don't insult my intelligence. No one usually gets that comfortable around someone like that: cooking for her, standing up others, and leaving money and sensitive information around someone after such a short time if you're not sleeping together. You've lied enough; no need to do that any longer."

"Yeah, I know."

"This, my friend, is karma. I am not rejoicing at your misfortune, but the way you treated me wasn't right. I would *never* steal from anyone. I have way too much class and integrity for that. I have a conscience. Everything I have, I've earned it. You chose the wrong woman, and now you are paying the price for it. Anyway, keep me posted on the outcome of everything. I also hope you know you can kiss that £300 you lent her good-bye as well."

I don't think he ever pressed charges against the woman for whatever reason, but he did cancel the credit cards she stole. He was shocked that I'd be so merciful toward him after how he stood me up and deceived me, but sometimes showing kindness to those who have wronged you may inspire a positive change in that person's life. I'd also grow to become his confidante despite him being seven years my senior. After it all went down, he became a more honest person, and every now and then we still touch base.

15 ISTANBUL MILLIONAIRE: MEHMET

During my final year in Europe, I decided to explore the history-rich city of Istanbul. I had no idea about the social norms or customs per se, but I knew I enjoyed the food back in London and that, based on pictures, it seemed like it would be a great experience. I remember this one hostel in particular had rave reviews, so I was sold very quickly on it and ended up staying there. The hostel owner was extremely nice and made sure his guests had a great time.

One day, I decided to grab a bite to eat for dinner. I soon learned that in Turkey when it rains, it really pours. At first I thought I could brave the storm, but then I realized I'd be soaked, even with an umbrella as the rain was even causing flooding the streets. I scoured the sidewalks to find a shed, long enough to shelter me from the downpour. Finally, I found this jewelry store shed outside for temporary shelter. Within five minutes of standing there, an older gentleman approached me.

"Excuse me, miss. You can sit on our couch and drink some apple tea if you'd like." (It is customary in Turkey to be offered apple tea by merchants and anyone extending hospitality.)

"No thank you, sir. I am waiting for the rain to stop so I can grab some dinner."

"It's going to be a *while* before the rain stops."

Part of my reluctance stemmed from the massive culture shock I experienced initially. As soon as a lot of the young men heard my American accent, they would treat me differently and not necessarily in a good way. Many watched a lot of American movies and perceived American women to be very loose. I was approached inappropriately several times and even flat out asked for sex even while dressed conservatively in jeans and a jacket. My negative experience led me to be apprehensive to accept any gestures from men.

About 45 minutes later, just as the older man had said, the rain was still pouring. Finally, I gave in and accepted the apple tea as I waited for the rain to stop. As an artist myself, I have always had a profound appreciation for people who are not only good at creating with their hands, but able to turn their talents into a profitable business as well.

"Wow, you made all of these?" I asked, pointing to the jewelry on display.

"Yes, and all by hand! Why don't you try on some of the necklaces?" He asked.

Clever sales pitch; offer me tea and shelter and ease into me purchasing goods. "Oh, well I would feel weird trying them on since I really didn't plan on buying anything." Before I knew it, he got up and placed a beautiful silver necklace with a turquoise pendant around my neck.

"Oh wow, it looks beautiful on you! Where are you from? My name is Deniz by the way."

I began to share my background with him. Soon, another older gentleman in his late fifties to early sixties arrived.

"I'd like you to meet my business partner, Mehmet."

We shook hands. "I can't believe this rain hasn't let up yet!" I said. "It's been an hour and half since I left my hostel. I might just chance it in the rain because I really think I should get going now!"

"So soon?" they both chimed.

"Well yeah, I left an hour and half ago to get dinner so I really should be on my way."

"Oh, well Mehmet here owns this entire building and the hotel and restaurant across the street," Deniz said.

"Let me give you a tour!" Mehmet said.

"I'm not too sure about that."

Mehmet insisted and went as far as saying in his culture it would be insulting for me to not take a tour. I figured since they were so nice to me and seemed old enough to be my dad, there would be no harm to it. "Okay, but it has to be quick because I need to get to the restaurant before dark." As Mehmet and I toured the place, I was in awe of how brilliant this man had to be to direct and design all these wonderful things. Our first stop was his rug store, where I saw beautiful handmade rugs purchased by clients all over the world. The next stop was the hotel, which was opulent and otherworldly. It had the best rooftop view of the entire city, and was right off of the ocean where they caught fresh fish.

"I'll tell you what. Why don't you just have dinner here tonight? Don't bother to go out in the rain," Mehmet suggested.

"Are you sure?"

"Yes, of course. This is nothing! What do you want?"

I wasn't too sure, so he asked his staff to bring out the sampler plates so I could try a little bit of everything. Over dinner, he told me his remarkable story of how he started off really poor as a child; he collected bottles off the streets and soon saved up enough to buy goods, such as clothes and carpets, in small quantities. He worked at a carpet shop for years. After working for an extended period of time, the shop owner was retiring and offered him the shop at a discount. It had done so well that soon he was able to open another carpet shop. He then linked up with

Deniz for the jewelry shop, and soon he had shops all over the United States, Middle East, and Turkey. He then decided to get into the luxury hotel and restaurant business.

I then spoke of my own entrepreneurial pursuits. He asked me where I was staying and I told him the name of the hostel that happened to be adjacent to his luxury hotel. He said if I'd like, I could stay in one of the rooms of his hotel for the remainder of my trip instead of having to share a room with others in a hostel. I respectfully turned down the offer and told him my hostel was great and already paid for. We said our good-byes, and that was it. He never once exhibited any kind of body language or behavior that would connote some kind of romantic interest. He was clearly a very affluent man, who I assumed had many women at his disposal.

The following day, the owner of my hostel said someone was on the line for me. I was genuinely perplexed because for the life of me, I couldn't figure out who it could be on the phone; none of my friends in Europe knew what hostel I was staying at, and we kept in touch via Skype and email anyway.

"For *me*?" I asked, completely puzzled. But I answered the call.

"Hello, this is Mehmet's assistant," the man said. "He wants to know if you could meet up with him in front of the hotel in the next hour."

"I'm sorry, pertaining to what now?" I replied.

"He'd rather talk about it in person."

"Okay, but I'm about to eat breakfast, so after that."

"You can eat while you're here; just come," he said.

As aforementioned, he never showed any explicit or implicit signs of romantic interest while we conversed so I thought it was completely innocent. This is obviously not something I'd recommend but since the owner of my hostel knew him personally, I felt somewhat at ease that if, God forbid, something went wrong, at least he'd be able to track it back to him. (The night before I was telling the owner how I met the renowned Mehmet while simply seeking shelter from the rain.)

We had breakfast, and then we did some sightseeing by the ocean. We also saw a live belly-dancing show—my first—and I even got to dance with one of the performers. I couldn't believe how hospitable he had been.

After the show, Mehmet said he needed to pick up something from his house. He said it might take a while to look for it, so I can come in for a glass of water or something. At first, we sat on his couch and he lamented about how he liked to live a simple life and how it's extremely hard for him to find friends who liked him for him, and not for what he had. He said dating was even worse. He had no kids and was never married (or so he claimed). He said he enjoyed my company and that I was easy to be around.

Next thing I knew, he took off his shirt while standing afar, revealing a wife beater and a ton of ink. *Holy crap! This dude is covered in tattoos!* I was a bit taken aback considering he was at least in his late fifties and came from a rather conservative culture. As he got closer, I realized what I was seeing weren't tattoos but curly black and gray hairs covering his entire body. They were at least three-inches long and coiled up. It was pretty gross. He sat next to me on the couch and gave me a kiss on my cheek. I was shocked. I let him know I wasn't that kind of girl and there would be "no sex in the champagne room." He then begged me to be his girlfriend, promising to be my sugar daddy.

"You'll get to travel all over the world with me! Please, let me spoil you!" He then revealed he had a sugar baby up until a few months prior; she was on the cusp of 21 and they had met when she was 18. I had no idea things would turn in that specific direction, so I told him to give me a day to think about it.

There was no way I was truly going to be anyone's

"sugar baby," but if he was nutso or thinking he'd have me by force that night (God forbid), it seemed smart to get the hell out of his place by any means. "Thinking about it" was just an attempt to buy time and temporarily appease him.

He drove us back to his hotel. He gave me his number to call him. Somehow, I think he got the picture it wasn't going to be that kind of party. He called my hostel again, and I wouldn't take the call. The creepiest part was when I stepped out to go to the town center, I saw six of his men on the corner; they were all staring at me, pacing back and forth. I would see them sporadically around town and my hostel too.

Oh my God. Is he going to stalk me now? Oh my God. He knows exactly where I am staying, I thought to myself. I was so freaked out I considered switching my hostel, but I only had one day left. I made nice with some of the other guests and only went out in groups on my final night. I never ever placed myself in that kind of position ever again, and am very grateful the situation didn't end on a bad note.

16 STOP & STARE: ROBIN

In my mid-teens, I met a gentleman by the name of Robin in a chat room. During my long, lackluster summers, he would keep me company on the phone. At first, he sent me a fake picture of this handsome male model. I became suspicious when all the pictures he sent seemed professional and staged; not a single one of them appeared to be an everyday photo. I asked to Skype, but he said he had no webcam (this was before the smartphone explosion). I then asked to speak with him on the phone and when I did, I didn't think his voice matched the pictures of the hot Latino guy he claimed to be. It was then his cover was blown. I confronted him about it, and he reluctantly confessed that it wasn't actually him. I then threatened to stop talking to him, and he immediately sent me the pictures of the real him. Albeit old and homely, we still had things to talk about and I figured I'd never meet him anyway. He was many years my senior; in fact, he was the same age as my parents. Although we spoke once or twice a week when I was bored, it wasn't until five years later that we actually got to meet in real life.

When I moved back to New York, we met for the

first time. I was a bit nervous about it but considering I emailed all his information to my best friend, I took the chance anyway. It was our first and last encounter. He took some modeling pictures of me as he was a teacher by day, photographer by night, and suggested we grab lunch at Carrabbas. One we arrived, I found our situation extremely comical. Everyone stopped and stared. On top of us being interracial, he had gray hair and was clearly over 20 years my senior. I've always had a baby face, and at 5'6" with a very slim frame, I probably appeared to be a teenager in many of the spectators' eyes.

"Why the hell is everyone staring?" Robin said in frustration.

"I dunno, Einstein. Take a wild guess!" I said sarcastically. I laughed to the point of tears rolling down my face. The waiter looked at us funny, and I had a permanent smirk on my face as she took our order.

Why the hell do I always find myself in these situations? Boredom strikes again! I said to myself. I couldn't believe he would be puzzled by such a glaringly obvious situation. He then asked me for a kiss at the table. I figured since I wasn't going to/didn't have to use tongue, maybe I could go through with it. I squinted my eyes tight as I quickly kissed this old man.

"You kissed me the way you would kiss one's grandma if she asked for some sugar," He said.

At that moment I lost it again, and my face turned beet red as the tears of laughter gushed down my cheeks. "I am sorry, but I've never kissed anyone as old as my dad before. It's a natural reaction."

As Robin walked me to the bus station, I then confirmed I wasn't the type who could date a man so much older than me, for love or money. It was weird and unnatural to me. We still keep in touch, but I had and have no plans of ever meeting up with him again!

17 THE FUNERAL DATE: KEN

One day, an older gentlemen contacted me about an opportunity on a companion rental site. Considering only one out of five people who contacted me on the site actually followed through, I tried not to get my hopes up too high whenever I received an email notification. I replied to his brief email about my availability for the weekend. Afterward, he gave me his number. I asked about the event details via text.

"I need an escort for a funeral on Saturday," he said.

Damn, I hate funerals. Dead bodies freak me out. Even human-hair extensions/wigs and certain prosthetics are enough to make me squeamish. I figured since it was highly likely I would have to go to other funerals in my life, I shouldn't shun the idea of attending this one in particular. When he called to get down to the nitty gritty, things got really bizarre.

"Hi, it's Ken."

"Hello, Ken. How are you?"

"Well, my mother died. I need a date for this funeral because I've been telling everyone about this girlfriend I've had for the past two years. They've never met her, and I am pretty sure both of my ex-wives are going to be there, and I need them to see me with a pretty young thing, such as yourself on my arm."

"So let me get this straight. Your mother just died, but you want to make sure at her funeral, your ex-wives are jealous, am I correct?"

"Yes! Both of them left me for another man. That left me in a lot of pain. People have been wondering why I've been single, so I've been telling everyone about my girlfriend, Melissa, who I've been seeing for the past two years, but they have never met her."

"I see. So family and co-workers have never met this Melissa girl? And you figured the most opportune time to introduce 'Melissa' was at your mother's funeral?"

"Yes. So can you do it?"

"Well, let's go over the details so it can sound believable."

I think the script devised was definitely soap opera-worthy. I was going to make my acting debut at a funeral where my pretend boyfriend was more concerned with how he was perceived by his exes than grieving the woman who carried him in her womb for nine months and raised him. He didn't seem to realize that I was posing questions in a certain way to provoke thought and self-reflection. I assumed him hearing how it sounded would give him a change of heart, but nope. I just couldn't fathom it on a personal level. It was incomprehensible to me that people actually thought like this in such a circumstance, but interestingly enough, this also added to my fascination. A new learning experience would be under my belt, and perhaps I was about to do one of the most interesting things I could ever and would ever do in my life.

"Okay, so describe Melissa. What does she do? Where does she live? How did you meet her? How long have you two been dating? All that good stuff."

"Oh, great questions! She works at a supermarket, she lives in Los Angeles, and we met kind of through her friend. One day, I went shopping at the supermarket, and I started talking to her friend who worked there. Then Melissa…or you…came over, and we started talking and exchanged numbers. We've been dating for over two years."

"Are you close with your family?"

"Yes."

"Then that last part doesn't work. There's no way anyone who is close to his family and living in close proximity would be dating someone for two years without the family ever meeting her. Doesn't sound believable. Let's say we were friends for over a year, but in a relationship for six months. You can then say you wanted to make sure you had a solid foundation and that things were going somewhere before formally introducing her. You've also got to understand people who've been dating longer will show it in their body language and the way they interact. The day of the funeral is the first day I will have ever met you, so we wouldn't be synchronized the way couples who have been together a while would be. I also just want you to get this straight: I am NOT your 'escort' by the modern-day definition. I am your only your date, nothing more. Got it?"

"Yes, okay. That's what I meant, just a date."

"And just to put it out there, we can hold hands, but there will be absolutely no kissing or any touchy feely. It would be weird and uncouth to be lovey dovey at a funeral anyway. It's just not appropriate."

"Okay, so what time should we meet?"

"To be honest, I'd prefer to meet you in person first, just to feel you out and break the ice. That way our first interaction isn't awkward to the point of being obvious."

"I'm afraid I won't have the time. It's already Thursday, and the funeral is Saturday."

We then discussed method of payment, etc. I had 48 hours to memorize my identity and his as well. I was praying he wasn't a wackadoodle, because the whole scenario in and of itself led me to think all his screws weren't tight. I just reasoned within myself to give him the benefit of the doubt. Maybe he had an unconventional way of grieving and/or maybe he was just emotionally immature.

I had a bit of anxiety as I arrived in front of his house, to ride with him to the funeral. Some of his family was already there in another car. *What if my cover is blown, and they get angry at me and I feel like crap? What if they think I'm some weird call girl?* I thought. We rode together, and I could tell Ken was nervous too. When we came out the car, I held his hand as we walked in. I breathed a sigh of relief when I saw no casket. I didn't even see an urn; just her image and a flower wreath. Some people's eyes were plastered on us, (the young/old couple) but unanimously, most people were grief-stricken and focused on their adieus to the deceased.

After the funeral, some family members and friends lingered in the church and that's when some people started to question me. I sensed it was time to split—and fast! One guy who was a close family friend seemed to smell something fishy; he asked questions like how we met, how long have we been dating, etc. The look in his eye and the tone in his voice showed more suspicion than curiosity. I excused myself to use the bathroom to escape the interrogation.

"So, did you see your ex-wives?"

"No, none of them came."

Oh. I could see the disappointment setting in, and perhaps a bit of common sense as well. The once enthusiastic and expectant man was hit with reality. This was a very silly and asinine idea. We went to the barbeque afterward (I was going to leave but figured it would be suspicious and disrespectful not to stay with the family). I tried to mainly sit by myself as to not provoke too many questions. As I sat with his niece and nephew (about 23 and 25), I admired how tactful and reverent they were in my presence. In my native culture and family, people have no issues with flat out asking someone, in front of their guest, what in the world are they thinking!

I told him it was time for me to go so then he walked me to his car. Ken said his nephew took him outside as they smoked cigarettes to ask what they hell was he doing with "that young girl." He then asked how did the billing work, and I gave him a discount under the circumstances. He said he might call me again for any other events, but I had a feeling he wouldn't; and he never did.

18 THE STAGE 5 CLINGER: LUKE

One day I decided to indulge in my newfound ethnic delight: papusas! Papusas are Salvadoran thick corn tortilla-like patties and are traditionally stuffed with beans, meat, cheese, or vegetables, served with pickled cabbage on the side. There was a papuseria about 15 minutes away from where I lived, so I figured it would be a good way to get some cardio in. As I entered the restaurant, I noticed a particular gentleman leaving it, and I didn't think anything of it. Afterwards, I was in the mood to check out a new shoe store up the street. On my way there, that same older man approached me and I had quick, feisty responses.

"I have a boyfriend, and he's crazy and I'm crazy too!" I belted, thinking this would scare him off.

"I just want to be your friend; can't we be friends?" he asked.

"No, because he'd better not be taking numbers from random women who approach him in the street."

"No harm in a friendship, love. I parked up the road, and my key is in the ignition; I can't tarry too long, but take my number?"

"NO! Have a nice day, sir."

He hastily scampered toward his vehicle with open windows and key in the car. I thought I had finally gotten rid of him, but he followed me into the shoe store 10 minutes later.

"See, I parked the car and came back *just for you*. How's your day? What do you want from this store? How about these shoes?" He held up a pair of shoes. They were gaudy gold metallic shoes with ugly ankle straps.

"Are you kidding me? Those are hideous! I already have something in particular in mind."

"How about these? These would look great on you!"

"No, they look cheap. Just because something *is cheap*, that doesn't mean it must *look cheap*." I thought being rude would deter him, but much to my chagrin, it didn't.

"Take my number. I live in Hollywood. I can take you shopping. Pick anything you want in the store."

"My mother and experience has taught me that there's no such thing as something for nothing. I highly doubt any rational person is going to just take a stranger shopping. You don't know diddlysquat about me."

"Yeah, your mom is right. I just want to take you out. We can paint the town tonight. I'll take you shopping, and we can go to the movies and then out for some sushi."

"I just ate dinner, and I told you I have a boyfriend."

"I have a good intuition about people, and I can tell you are a great person already. Take my number," he said as he slipped it into my purse.

I finally found a pair of shoes I deemed cute and went to the cash register, card in my hand to pay for them. He literally pushed my hand out of the way and told the cashier not to accept my money. Just to make it clear, they weren't Louboutins, but rather a $14 pair of sandals. I would have vehemently refused had it been an expensive pair of shoes. He was so proud of his purchase. He began to tell me about his ex-girlfriend that had left him three months prior. Apparently when they had met, she lied about her age. She was 18, but told him she was 21. He was about 31 when they had met. According to him, she confessed about six months into their relationship after they had begun living together. Why he would feel it was appropriate or prudent to tell a new "love interest" about his ex-girlfriend is beyond me, but this little detail would prove to be a critical piece to the puzzle I would later solve.

He told me to call him so he would have my number as well. I dialed his number in front of him but didn't let it ring so he wouldn't have my number. Fortunately for me, he had left his phone in the car. He was also from New York, and New Yorkers, from my experience, easily sense tactics to get out of giving one's number. I really didn't want to contact him, but I figured it would rude to accept something without at least saying thank you. I must admit he was the most persistent man I had ever encountered in person, *ever*. He should have been a salesman because he would have done very well.

I really didn't have a boyfriend, and I figured he'd be an interesting person to hang out with, even if it would be just once. I had plans to leave L.A. soon anyway (which I made clear), and it had been a few months since I had gone out on a date. The next day, I thanked him via text and by the following day, we solidified plans for a date that Friday, but he asked me something that was the second most ridiculous proposal anyone has ever made within only three days of knowing me.

"Where's the restaurant?" Luke asked.

"It's called Boiling Crab. The address is 3333 Lonesome Lane, Los Angeles."

"Oh okay, what's the number?"

"You know you can Google this stuff, right?" I said.

"Anyway, what time are you getting off on Friday?"

"I don't know yet. Why, beautiful?"

"To time the meet up. Since it's a holiday weekend, my

boss will probably let me off early."

"What meet up?"

"Uhhh…our date?"

"Come stay with me," he said out of nowhere. "I know you will say something feisty, so go ahead, say it!"

"You must be out of your mind!"

"You will save money. Just try it!"

"On what?"

"Rent. You buy the food, I pay the rent."

"Surely you must be joking, or perhaps my ears are deceiving me?" I asked.

"Seriously, NO!" I shouted. "Wipe off your lip because you are talking shit! I don't know if you take me for a half idiot or a buffoon! I don't have time for it!"

"Okay, I respect you! I don't take you for anything. Anyway, are you still coming to Malibu this weekend?"

I could not believe after knowing me for three days and barely even having a 30-minute conversation he would suggest moving in! He didn't know *anything* about me! My hygiene, how responsible I am (or am not), how much I make, if I'm completely off my rocker, if I take commitments seriously, etc. Then I started to connect the dots. He moved into a swanky part of town with his ex-girlfriend and because she had left, he was probably stuck with rent he could barely afford. He was desperately scouring for assistance. He texted me *every single day* for over a month, despite my insisting that there would never be an "us." He even went as far as saying he loved me. I never replied to his barrage of texts. Finally, I got fed up and threatened to contact the police. I was freaked out by his harassing behavior. That's when he finally got the hint. I'm thankful he never saw my license plate, let alone where I lived. I then learned how critical having a Google Voice number is in the initial stages of contact with a new guy. I wished him luck with his search for a roommate. Good riddance!

19 IT DOESN'T REALLY MATTER: DANIEL

After an extended break from dating, I decided to go on my first date with Daniel. My coworkers raved about this site called OkCupid that somehow, despite all of my online dating exploits, I had never heard of before. I figured as long as the quality of people were better than some other sites, I'd be down for it. Within minutes of putting up my profile, I received several emails, but the thing about Daniel's email that caught my eye was his sense of humor. He didn't come off as desperate like many others, but rather, a cool, calm, and collected man. It also didn't hurt that I loved the way his eyes squinted as he smiled.

We Skyped to avoid a catfish situation, and he actually laughed at me when I told him about my first online experience and how it made me Skype before every first meeting. He complimented my outfit, and we both stood up and walked around to ensure the other we were as "normal" as possible (physically, that is).

Our first date was at a diner/dive bar. Daniel was a bit late, which wasn't exactly the best first impression. When he called me, for some reason (I don't know why), he thought I was upset. I really wasn't. I am not sure if Daniel read too many self-help/psychology books, but his projecting started to irritate me within minutes of us meeting.

"You seemed a bit upset when I called. Did you interpret me being a bit late as me not respecting your time? Is that what it is? Did that hurt your feelings?"

"No, I was a bit annoyed at first, yes, but I'm not holding on to that. To be honest, we're both here now, and that's in the past. Let's focus on here and now. I always speak my mind and let it go."

"Are you *sure*? I just feel some tension."

"There's no 'tension,' but what will eventually start to aggravate me is if you continue to assume how I feel and constantly imply that I am not being honest about my feelings and thoughts. You should respect them and give me the benefit of the doubt." Then I politely changed the topic.

We ended up having so much fun for the rest of the date. I played some YouTube videos of people falling and busting their behinds; I know it's slightly sadistic but I find that extremely funny. He found the fact I found it funny, hilarious in and of itself. He also said I had an infectious laugh. We planned our next date, which would last a full weekend.

For our next adventure, we went to a party and I ended up sleeping over. We didn't kiss until the second day. We laughed up a storm and had a lot more fun than I had had in a while. I asked him important questions about intimacy and his views on online dating. He told me he didn't have sex outside of relationships, and I let him know I shared his perspective. He asked me by the end of the second day to be his girlfriend. I politely declined as I felt I needed to go out a bit more before committing. He told me he could respect that.

We made plans for the next weekend, and we also had a blast. I cooked him a curry dish. Daniel picked up the chicken with his bare hands and wiped the sauce off in a napkin. He then touched my white shirt. I freaked out. I wasn't trying to be rude, but I thought it'd be obvious not to touch curry and then someone's white blouse. That seemed to upset him a bit. I apologized for overreacting and hurting his feelings. I then began to realize how emotionally fragile he was.

We ended up taking things a bit further that weekend, but we didn't sleep together. I saw him hastily grabbing some condoms.

"What are those for?" I inquired.

"Oh, well just in case we have sex."

I told him there would be none of that so soon and outside the context of a relationship. He claimed he understood, and we fell asleep in each other's arms. The next day, the 180-degree turn began.

"Okay, now that we've spent two full weekends together and have started getting more physical, I'll take you up on your girlfriend offer," I said. "I don't want to be kissing multiple people I go out with, so now I think it's appropriate. I don't exactly think we need to put titles on things, but let's at least pause our profiles until we see if we can make something work."

"I don't know," Daniel said, shaking his head. "I mean, a lot of women are showing interest in me. From work to online."

I couldn't help but laugh. "Okay, but just seven days ago you asked me to be your girlfriend, no? I have plenty of men pursuing me as well, so what's your point?"

"I'm not saying no, but I need more time to think about it."

"Um. Ok."

A wise man once told me a long time ago to beware of people who profess love and/or rush into relationships too quickly; these are the same people who fall out of the love and change their minds the quickest. He was correct. I needed time to process my feelings, so we went out for lunch. When we came back, we had one of the most pointless conversations ever.

"So there's something else I need to discuss with you," he said. I knew it was most likely regarding his ex-girlfriend since when she called, he walked out of the room. I know it's not the best thing to do, but when he went to the bathroom, I went through his phone and saw her text messages to him up to six weeks prior. She told him she wanted to sleep with him. He didn't flirt in return but just replied with a myriad of "lols" following each desperate plea for him to sex her down. She even went as far as saying she recently had a dream that he was "killing her vagina," which I found hilarious quite frankly.

"So my ex-girlfriend's job is opening up two locations near by me. She lives a little out of the way, but she asked if she can stay over. If she can't, she understands."

"Okay, so what's the issue?"

"Well, I wanted to know how you feel about it."

"To be honest, it makes me a bit uncomfortable. Although you said it's been six months since you've last been intimate, I don't think it's appropriate, couch or not. She did say, after all, 'if she can't, she understands.' What I deduce from that statement is that she has alternatives, so I don't see why she cannot just utilize them."

"Hmm. Well that's something to think about."

"I mean, am I being rational? Is that a plausible assumption?"

"Yes, but she's my friend; I would feel weird not helping a friend out in need when they can just crash on my couch, and nothing would happen. I guess I will decide by the end of the week."

"Well you asked how I felt, so there it is. Anyway, I guess by the end of the week you'll make your decision."

"Okay."

Little did he know, I had already read the text messages. She was clearly coming on to him. I knew what was up. I couldn't see how he could be adamant about the innocence of the situation when she clearly had ulterior motives. I couldn't take the suspense anymore, so I called him the next day.

"Did you make a decision?"

"Well, what would you say if I told you I would host her? Would that mean we couldn't continue seeing each other?"

"Okay, well what if I told you I don't want her to stay over?"

"Well, I don't think we're at the point to be laying down these kinds of restrictions. I mean we just started seeing each other."

69

"Look, I am not going to play these games, okay? For the love of God, I am asking this question in complete and utter sincerity since I'm struggling to comprehend: why did you even ask my opinion? She could have slept over, and I wouldn't have even known about it. Based on your rationale, I shouldn't really know about it since my opinion and our status is seemingly inconsequential at the moment."

"Well, I just didn't think it would be right to have her sleep over and not tell you anything."

"Okay, so when you asked me to be your girlfriend a mere week ago, I mean, what was the point of that? And once again, why ask me how I felt if you were going to disregard it anyway? It sounds like you've already made up your mind as to what you're going to do. I think you should do what you feel like doing. I don't want anyone making a decision under duress. I just don't appreciate being asked something if you never were going to genuinely take it into consideration. Perhaps you should have said your ex is sleeping over, thought I should know and left it at that—a statement and not a question."

From that moment forward, everything he said was akin to Charlie Brown teacher's "womp womp womp womp womp." My ears and mind refused to process it. To be honest, I don't remember the last part of that conversation but I remember getting so annoyed and frustrated that I just hung up the phone on him. It had been years since I last did that, but I just couldn't take the silly answers and the senseless situation. I then, of course, apologized via text for being immature and disrespectful by hanging up the phone. He accepted this apology and vowed to keep in touch, but of course, we never did.

THE FINALE

So there you have it, a collection of some of the craziest dating experiences you will probably ever hear. I have no idea what consistently attracted some of these people to me. The bright side of things is that now I truly know what I want (and don't want), as well as what I have to offer. I've also mellowed out a lot, matured immensely, and dated men closer to my age range. Although it can be boring at times, at least it's normal. Only time will tell if normal is overrated. Thank you for reading!

www.ingramcontent.com/pod-product-compliance
Lightning Source LLC
Chambersburg PA
CBHW060040040426
42331CB00032B/1829